651.3 Lillegard, Dee
LI
        I can be a
        secretary

$13.27

DATE			
AG 01 '91			
OT 07 96			
AU 08 '97			
OCT 08 '97			
AY 07 '99			
MY 04 01			
AG 04 '08			

I CAN BE A SECRETARY

By Dee Lillegard

Prepared under the direction of Robert Hillerich, Ph.D.

 CHILDRENS PRESS ®

CHICAGO

Lillegard, Dee.
    I can be a secretary.
    Includes index.
    1. Secretaries—Juvenile literature. I. Title.
HD8039.S58L55   1987   651.3'741'02373   86-29947
ISBN 0-516-01907-4

PICTURE DICTIONARY

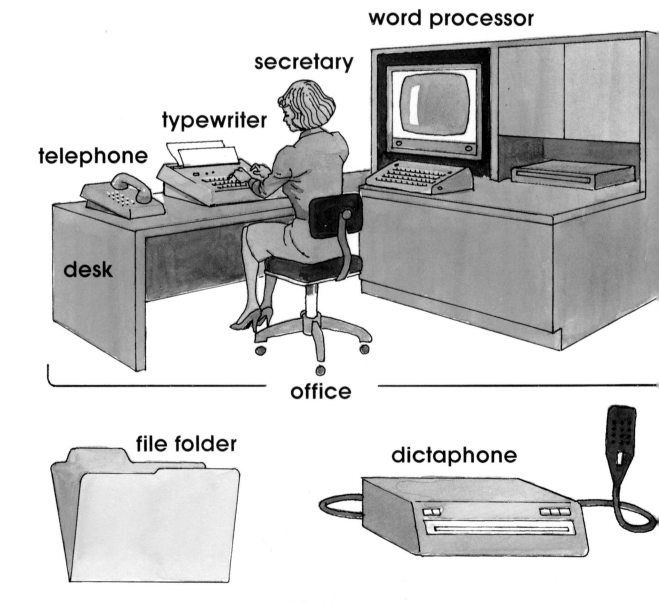

secretarial pool

typing

bookkeeping

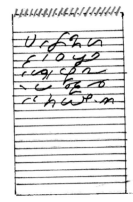

shorthand

calculator

copy machine

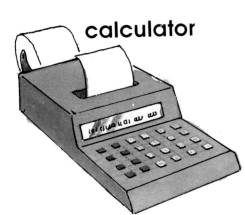

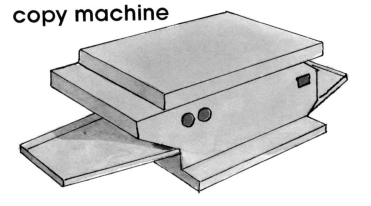

Secretaries enjoy their jobs because they know how valuable they are.

HELP WANTED
SECRETARY to handle correspondence, phones. Must have positive attitude. Lots of responsibility. Exciting opportunity for right person.

Ads like this appear in newspapers everywhere, every day.

Secretaries are in great demand. There is even a Secretary's Day, like Mother's Day and Father's Day, to show how much secretaries are appreciated.

Big companies could not exist without good secretaries.

Every office needs a secretary. Every kind of business needs a secretary. What do secretaries do that is so important to so many people?

Secretaries are never far
from the telephone.

Secretaries handle
office communications.
They keep records,
answer letters, and
handle telephone calls.
They set up meetings and
appointments, and often
solve problems among
other office workers.

Secretaries save their employers from many kinds of problems and interruptions. A good secretary helps a company to run smoothly. But things don't always run smoothly for secretaries!

Secretaries make life easier for their employers.

Sometimes everything
seems to happen at
once. An important letter
must be typed. The
phone keeps ringing.
Visitors come into the
office.

Good secretaries are pleasant,
kind, and helpful,
as well as businesslike.

Secretaries have to be
able to handle a wide
variety of jobs—and
interruptions. But they
must always be polite.

Did you know that the first secretaries in history were men? Kings had secretaries who handled important business for them. Now, leaders of countries have assistants such as a secretary of defense and a secretary of agriculture.

Secretaries may work in schools or churches, in small shops, or in big office buildings. Some secretaries have an office of their own. Some work in a large, open area with many other

Secretaries use a variety of office machines.

secretaries. This is called a secretarial pool.

secretarial pool

Secretaries usually have a desk, a typewriter, and a telephone of their own. Their tools include pencils and pens, notebooks,

telephone typewriter

desk

word processor

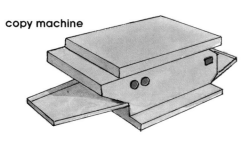
copy machine

file folder

and file folders. They should also have a calendar for writing down appointments and a good dictionary. Secretaries in most offices today also use a copy machine and a word processor.

The word "secretary" first meant "one who could be trusted with secrets." A secretary had to be trustworthy and have good judgment. That is still true. But secretaries today have to know more than "how to keep a secret."

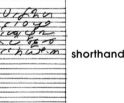

Some secretaries study typing, shorthand, and bookkeeping in high school. They may begin

typing

bookkeeping

shorthand

working as typists or file
clerks and move up to
being secretaries.

Others go to college or
business school to study
secretarial science. They
take courses in office

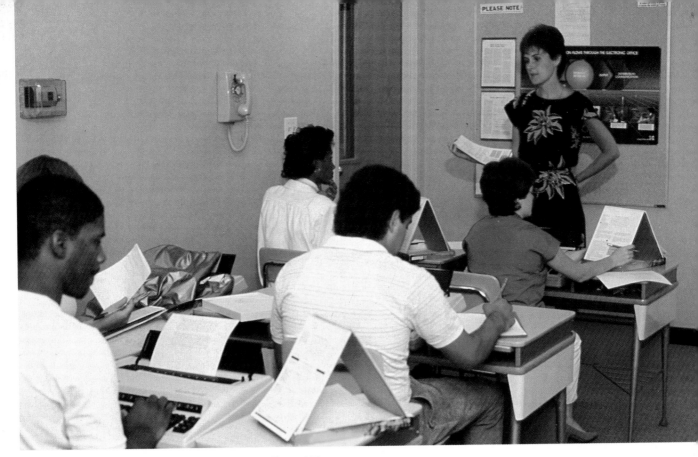

Business colleges teach valuable office skills.

systems, business English, and word processing, as well as typing and shorthand. They learn to use a dictaphone and a calculator. Many also study accounting.

dictaphone

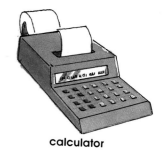

calculator

A typing class

There are special
classes for legal and
medical secretaries. And
secretaries who want to
work for international
organizations may need
to learn one or more
foreign languages.

Supervisors giving instructions
to secretaries

Secretaries have to
work quickly and
accurately. They must be
good at spelling,
punctuation, and
grammar. They must be
able to follow instructions.

19

But they must also work well on their own.

Secretaries have to know how to behave and how to dress on the job. Employers like their secretaries to have a professional and businesslike appearance.

Most secretaries work
eight hours a day, five
days a week. But there
are many part-time and
temporary jobs available.
"Temps," or temporary
secretaries, fill in for
permanent secretaries
who are on vacation or
away from the office for
some other reason.

An executive of a college and his secretary

Temps work in a variety
of places and situations.
Secretaries are needed
in every industry, from
bottle-making to movie-
making. And there are

Secretaries are needed wherever their employers do their business.

many secretarial jobs in
government. There is sure
to be a need for
secretaries in any field
that interests you.

Secretaries learn a lot about the businesses they work for. They are an important part of business management. Many secretaries become administrative assistants or executive secretaries. Some are promoted to higher management positions.

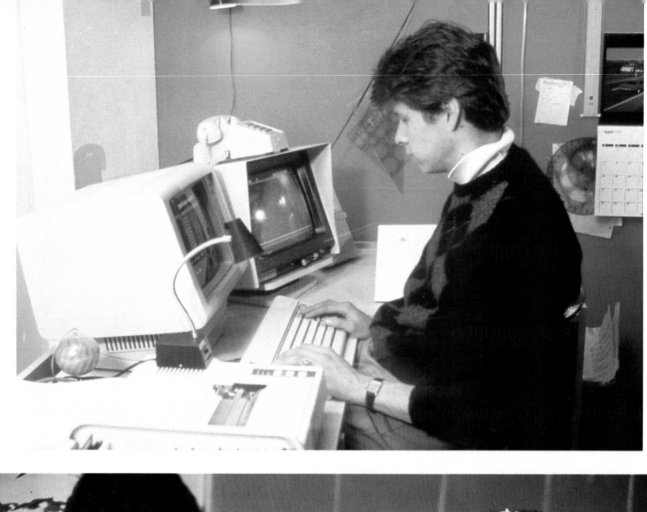

Secretarial experience has helped many people open their own businesses or run their households more efficiently. No one has ever regretted having secretarial skills!

Being a secretary is challenging and rewarding. Best of all, a secretary is *help wanted—and needed!*

WORDS YOU SHOULD KNOW

accounting (uh • KOWN • ting)—the system of recording a company's money matters

attitude (AT • ih • tood)—how a person feels and thinks about something

bookkeeping (BOOK • keep • ing)—recording the amounts of money a business takes in and spends

correspondence (kor • uh • SPON • dence)—letters

dictaphone (DICK • tuh • fone)—a tape recorder into which an employer speaks so that a secretary can later type what was spoken, usually a letter or a report

file clerk (FILE CLERK)—a person whose job is to file business papers and keep them in good order

grammar (GRAM • er)—the correct use of words in making sentences

interruption (in • ter • UP • shun)—the act of breaking in on someone's conversation or activity

legal (LEE • gul)—having to do with law or lawyers

office (OFF • us)—the central place where a business is run and where its records are kept

punctuation (punk • choo • AY • shun)—the marks used with written language, such as commas and periods

secretarial pool (sek • ruh • TEH • ree • ul POOL)—a group of secretaries who work in one large, open space

shorthand (SHORT • hand)—a method of speed-writing

temporary (TEM • puh • reh • ree)—lasting for a short time

INDEX

PHOTO CREDITS

ABOUT THE AUTHOR

Dee Lillegard has been an executive secretary, administrative assistant, and office manager. She is the author of many books for children and finds her secretarial skills invaluable to her as a writer.